Jungle Animals

BATS

By Rob Ryndak

Gareth Stevens
PUBLISHING

Please visit our website, www.garethstevens.com. For a free color catalog of all our high-quality books, call toll free 1-800-542-2595 or fax 1-877-542-2596.

Library of Congress Cataloging-in-Publication Data

Ryndak, Rob.
Bats / by Rob Ryndak.
p. cm. — (Jungle animals)
Includes index.
ISBN 978-1-4824-1745-6 (pbk.)
ISBN 978-1-4824-1746-3 (6-pack)
ISBN 978-1-4824-1744-9 (library binding)
1. Bats — Juvenile literature. I. Title.
QL737.C5 R96 2015
599.4—d23

First Edition

Published in 2015 by
Gareth Stevens Publishing
111 East 14th Street, Suite 349
New York, NY 10003

Editor: Ryan Nagelhout
Designer: Katelyn E. Reynolds

Photo credits: Cover, p. 1 Craig Dingle/E+/Getty Images; p. 5 nattanan726/Shutterstock.com; pp. 7, 24 (wings) Nathape/Shutterstock.com; pp. 9, 24 (colony), 11, 13 Ivan Kuzmin/Shutterstock.com; p. 15 belizar/Shutterstock.com; pp. 17, 24 (teeth) Gunter Ziesler/Photolibrary/Getty Images; p. 19 Carol Farneti Foster/Oxford Scientific/Getty Images; p. 21 Rexford Lord/Photo Researchers/Getty Images; p. 23 Oxford Scientific/Getty Images.

Printed in the United States of America

CPSIA compliance information: Batch #CW15GS: For further information contact Gareth Stevens, New York, New York at 1-800-542-2595.

Contents

Bats are wild animals.

Bats can fly!
They have
very strong wings.

They live in big groups.
These are called colonies.

Bats have very big ears.
They have great hearing.

They find food
in the dark.

Some bats drink blood.

These bats have very sharp teeth.

They bite down
and drink blood.

Bats like to bite horses and cows.

Sometimes they bite pigs!

Words to Know

colony

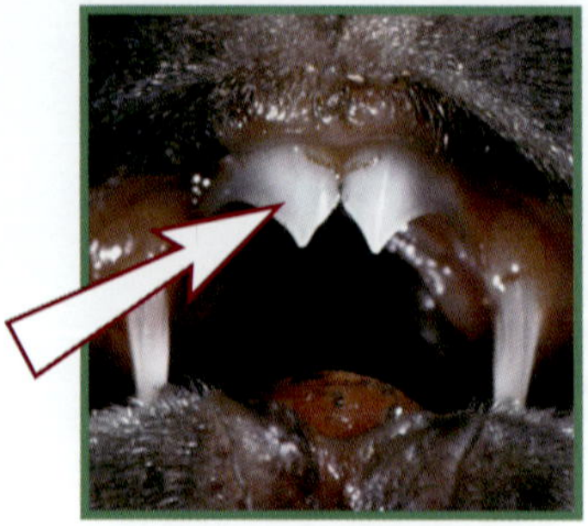
teeth

wings

Index